Echoes from the Valley

ERNIE ANDERSON

Copyright © 2021 Ernie anderson.

All rights reserved. No part of this book may be reproduced, stored, or transmitted by any means—whether auditory, graphic, mechanical, or electronic—without written permission of both publisher and author, except in the case of brief excerpts used in critical articles and reviews. Unauthorized reproduction of any part of this work is illegal and is punishable by law.

ISBN: 978-1-949735-53-6 (sc)
ISBN: 978-1-949735-56-7 (hc)
ISBN: 978-1-949735-71-0 (e)

Because of the dynamic nature of the Internet, any web addresses or links contained in this book may have changed since publication and may no longer be valid. The views expressed in this work are solely those of the author and do not necessarily reflect the views of the publisher, and the publisher hereby disclaims any responsibility for them.

OTHER BOOKS BY ERNIE ANDERSON:

The Release of the Albatross

The Return of the Albatross

Whispers from the Hills

Train to Destiny

This book is dedicated to the US Military
for all of those who are now serving
and who have served in the past.
We salute you!

Contents

Ghost Town 1
The Tulip 3
To Find Your Calling 4
Poor Dreamer 5
Unconditional Love 6
The Paradox of Fire and Water 7
The Morning After 8
Memories 9
Abundant Wealth 10
Tennessee Christmas 11
The Wings of the Wind 13
Soaring Spirit 14
Libby 15
Mother's Love 17
Count the Cost 19
Do the Things We Should 21
Prisoner of Love 22
In Honor of Martha Stuart Oden 23
Do I Want to Fly? 24
"Deep Water" 25
Hope Realized 26
Play the Hand You Were Dealt 27
If I Were an Octopus 28
The Want of Wings 29
Who Are You? 30
Sailors We Are 31
Timeless Beauty 32
Away with me to Scotland 33
Ultimate Love 34
What am I? 35
Morning 36
Who am I? 37

Hail to Covington High	38
Happy Fathers Day to Me	40
Come Boldly	41
The Dawn of Life	42
New Life	43
Dawn	44
Kindred Slave	45
Until	46
Loving You	47
The Beacon of your Love	48
The Window of Your Soul	49
True Love	50
The Garden	51
My Prayer	52
Nothing Left to Lose or Gain	53
The Horrors of War	54
The Effect of Music	56
Searching Eye	57
Trade In	58
Gone and Yet Here	60
Whispers from the Hills	61
Chance or Fate	62
Memories that Won't Die	63
Regret	64
My Trouble	65
I'll Love you in Any Season	66
Resurrected Slave	67
Madonna	69
The Dawn	70
Help Another Rose to Bloom	71
The Mighty Oak	72
Unknown Soldier	73
I Just Came to Dance	74
Footprints	75
Grandmother's Timeless Beauty	76
Music	77
Live Above It	78

If you try to hide, I will find you...79
Hope Realized 80
Hailey's Comet 81
I Can Hear Your Love Calling..82
The Window of Your Soul 83
The Passion of the Poet 84
Love Enough for Tomorrow...85
The Birth...86
The Power of a Smile 87
Completed Book 88
The Ant 89
Thoughts of Spring...90
The Moon..91
Your Love..92

Ghost Town

It was a sunny day in June and there in that sleepy town I found that there was no one else around. From the restaurant no odor filled the skis; neither did coal dust from the coal yard fill my eyes. What manner of town is this I implore, as I just then began to explore? Armed with my curious mind I muttered about, stopped short and elevated my ear, what is that I hear, was that a bang or a shout? Returning to my search I took a look therein that town in every cranny and in every nook. Though look I did, none could I find, an ointment or a salve of another kind that would calm my nerves and ease my mind.

What manner of town is this, when clearly there is something amiss? I've searched this town now high and low and no one has appeared neither above nor below. Down the road trod I to take yet another look, fully baffled now by no sound, continued I to look around to see if anything therein could be found in the depths of this empty town. A futile search I could plainly see, I'll take my leave now from this town, but no ticket master there was around, though I was fully in agreement now with me. No train was there upon the absent track and though the bus stop was there, the bus it did lack. No cab was found there in that town, the city limits there within and whats more than that had probably never been a cab therein. I could forget the cab ride from that town so I continued to walk and look around that town and decided that if I could not ride that I would search for me a place to rest and hide. Was that a jab I felt there in my side? Since I am here now in this place and stare this absence square in the face, it seems that I'm the only one now here; I thought I just heard a laugh or jeer?

Is this place then filled with a ghost and of the population I am the most, I should be gone now from this place I said as I began to sweat my face got red. I've been here now for some time and found nothing yet as I said, I thought I heard a bell or chime, if I stay here I'll end up dead.

Though I wished to take my leave, something then just pulled my sleeve and as I looked around to see, nothing stood there watching me. Or was the nothing in my mind and something stood there just behind, some presence of another kind, playing tricks now on my mind. What was that behind that blind?

Anxious was I now to go, where the exit was I did not know, so wonder about again I did, trying to leave this box without a lid. If ever my leave I can take, the dust off my feet I will surly shake, I'll never again return to this place, this town never again will see my face. Was that a lady there, dressed in lace?

Now as the cloudy sky got dark, I walked across the empty park and thought this town one big pain, when just then it began to rain, I went for cover down the lane. Was that the rattle of a chain?

I knew right then I'd made a mistake and from the lane my leave I would take if I could only find the door, I'd leave this lane and return no more and I would head straight to the shore. Was that someone peeking around that door?

And now this story I must end before its the longest story thats been, I could go on for days on end, but then, would you remain my friend? From this ghost town I now escape and only memories do I take. Never again will I return, to the town that I had found, where I wondered a while and looked around and counting all nothing was found. I leave you now to heal in time from the feel of the willys running up your spine. When you hear the chain rattle in the night, have no fear or take up fright. Or if you see a lady dressed in lace, her eyes appearing only, without a face, Don't run away and hide, should you feel a jab there in your side, Remember this and you will glean that things are not always what they seem,

In the town we leave the ghosts we've seen and now wake up from this dream.

ERNEST L. ANDERSON
6/20/03

The Tulip

The sleeping tulip, lying dormant throughout the winter in its underground home, begins to stir and becomes energized as the warm rays of the sun magnetically draw its arched back toward the surface of the earth. Finally, yielding to the warmth, the growing tulip penetrates the earth; bowing first, so deeply, that its head is the last to appear before it slowly stands, and recovering from it's bow, remains triumphantly at attention with outstretched petals fully opened, as if in praise and thanksgiving to the sun, for releasing it from its long captivity. We reap the harvest of the tulip's labor with our eyes as we gaze upon the beauty of its petals and as the honey bee partakes of its sweet pollen. The tulip has, once again, taken its place in the spring garden and enriches the lives of all who observe her.

ERNEST L. ANDERSON
1/15/04

To Find Your Calling

Happy is the one
who in life has found,
the purpose and reason
they hang around.

When work is there pleasure
and passion their way,
they work hard as they can
with the few hours in a day.

When at last they lay down
to rest in their bed,
the full day of work
parades through their head.

They ponder the pleasure
work brought for a while,
then quietly roll over
go to sleep with a smile.

ERNEST L. ANDERSON
1/10/04

Poor Dreamer

Cry not for the poor dreamer
who could go but half way up,
Neither feel sorry for him,
seeing the emptiness of his cup.

Let your tears be shed for another
and your sorrow upon him fall,
the one, out of fear, who saved his full cup
and followed no dream at all.

Like the flight of the mighty eagle
the dreamers' first try was poor,
Soon, with determination and courage
his spirit with eagles would soar.

Pity the one who grips the limb
whose fear won't let him try,
He flaps his wings, but can't let go
No one will hear his sigh.

ERNEST L. ANDERSON
1/09/04

Unconditional Love

The old man, in his haste, hit the dog with the stick and chased him away. The dog retreated sulkily with his tail between his legs, as he glanced back occasionally at his master. Lying under the tree at a safe distance the dog observed the man's every move and his eyes never left the man. Throwing the stick in the woods, the man seated himself in the chair on the porch and began to rock. Considering his actions, he heard the voice of his conscience and glanced at the dog. The glance brought the dogs ears immediately to attention. Extending his hand toward the dog brought him to his feet, as he gave his attention fully to the man. The snapping of the man's fingers caused the dog to come running, happily wagging his tail, as he licked the man's hand in forgiveness. As I pondered the scene, I thought, *what can I learn from this unconditional love exhibited by the dog and his quickness to forgive?*

ERNEST L. ANDERSON
1/07/04

The Paradox of Fire and Water

How comforting to sit warmly before a cozy fireplace when it is snowing and 15 degrees outside.

Or to lie on the beach and be soothed by the rhythmic play of the waves as they unendingly wash the shore.

How devastating then, as the raging fire consumes what it took a lifetime to build, as you watch your house, hopes, and dreams go up in smoke.

How stressful to stand and watch your house being swept away in the flooding waters of the river after it had received three days of continuous rain which its banks could not contain.

ERNEST L. ANDERSON
1/07/04

The Morning After

Then, the morning after, it makes you wonder.
Did he think they wouldn't make any more after yesterday?

He drank like a law was going into effect, and that would be the last day drinking would be allowed.

As you watched him take his aspirin and hold his head, it makes you wonder. Was there a raging fire inside of him that he was trying to extinguish?

One benefit, I suppose, is the fact that, surely, he will feel better as the day wears on. He must feel better, so he can make happy hour this evening.

ERNEST L. ANDERSON
1/07/04

Memories

You can't run away from a memory
It will find you every time
It'll search every dark corner
every recess of your mind.

Then it will show you
the picture that it found,
Will you smile and be happy?
or will it cause you to wear a frown?

Take each memory as it comes
place them on the back shelf,
They no longer belong to you
since they happened to someone else.

No one remains the same
We're not who we were back then
but when you see the picture of your memories
May they embrace you as your friend.

ERNEST L. ANDERSON
1/04/04

Abundant Wealth

There is one thing for sure under the sun,
Time moves on and waits for none.
Some comfort is found from the words of the sage,
We all can still learn, at any age.

Reach for the stars, and pursue your dreams,
Expand your vision, by volumes and reams.
Contentment is present, not something you find
Under wrong thoughts, you need expelled from your mind.

Happiness is here, not way over there
Shielded from sight by your burdens and care.
Change your attitude, about fortune and fame
Then join the winners who play life's game.

Watch the words you say, and in yourself believe
Remember what you give, you shall also receive,
Be generous with others, and thus to yourself,
Your heart will overflow with the abundance of wealth.

ERNEST L. ANDERSON
12/29/03

Tennessee Christmas

Twas the night before Christmas, when all through the house
Pa looked for his boots, while chewing a piece of souse.
His stockings he found in the living room chair
Right where Rover had placed them there.

The boys were all sawing, logs in their beds
While visions of new rifles danced in their heads.
Ma slept in her kerchief, Pa donned his fur cap
Everyone, except him, was in for a nap.

Then out toward the still there rose such a clatter,
Pa went out the door to see what was the matter.
Off through the woods, he flew like a flash
to check on the progress of the bubbling sour mash.

He could see by the moonlight, reflecting on the snow
It was just like midday in the valley below,
When, what to his sleepy eyes did appear,
He thought it was a revenuer, though it wasn't clear.

He had his hounds with him, there was Prancer and Vixen.
Two Pa hadn't seen, then Donder and Blitzen.
They came up the valley, to the top of the hill
Then seeing the smoke, they headed for the still.

The dry leaves betrayed them, and gave them away
Pa followed at a distance, as they went on their way.
Up the high mountain, the hounds just flew
with the man in tow, Pa followed them too.

His eyes---- how they twinkled, when his pipe he did fill
They had finally arrived, in sight of Pa's still,
He drooled from his mouth, and his face was aglow
They walked to the still through the new fallen snow.

Speaking not a word, he went right to work
He filled two mason jars, then turned with a jerk,
Pa raised the barrel skyward, as his shotgun he fired
The way they all scattered, gave no hint they were tired.

They ran down the hill, as the dogs gave a howl
On past the barn and the big fat sow,
Not knowing where to run, just away from here
That old man and his dogs, and two bottles of cheer.

Pa got to the still, saw everything was all right
The man and his dogs were now out of sight,
He filled all the jars, as the batch he did run
Then took a quart to his wife, and one for each son.

They all wore a big smile, and their spirts did soar
when they saw the arm full, Pa brought through the door,
The old man had his squeesings, no harm had been done
"Merry Christmas to all, it had all been great fun.

ERNEST L. ANDERSON
12/16/03

The Wings of the Wind

When the fire of life has burned most of your tomorrows
leaving ashes where hopes and promises once grew,
Where is the place of solace found for charred sorrows?
Where can the wings be found, and your flight renew?

Fly upon the wings of the wind (Psalms 18.10)
Returning in your mind to the days of your youth,
When the unknowns of tomorrow were your friend
In days when hopes and dreams were not aloof.

Mount up with wings as eagles and do not faint (Isa. 40.31)
Run weariless, the running being its own reward,
Find the beauty where the present cannot taint.
Hear within your spirit, the resounding chord.

Once there, in that place, just you and Him
the refreshing breeze blowing through your hair,
Your renewed spirit arrives on the wings of the wind
which has blown away your every care.

ERNEST L. ANDERSON
12/27/03

Soaring Spirit

May the breath of life breathe on you with the power of gentle strength,

Moving under your wings and lifting you upward to heights not seen in your most extreme imagination.

Once there, exciting your senses, may you be filled with unspeakable joy, as your thirsty eyes drink in the surrounding beauty and as your ears are filled with the sounds of the choir of the heavens.

Basking there for a time, then gently drifting yet higher to places never seen or imagined before. Renewing your strength, energizing your spirit and causing you to stretch far beyond former fences and boundaries of your creativity. Thus, now able to give freely and to share the gift you have received with the realization that it is yours alone to give. Then and only then will you sleep.

ERNEST L. ANDERSON
10/25/03

Libby

There was a young lady in Fairlea
who was as sweet as she could be,
She daily went about her work
staying as busy as a bee.

Some said that around the edges
that she was a little bit rough,
Mom and I always knew better
we never listened to that huff.

Nothing kept her from her patients
Neither rain, or snow or sleet,
You could always count on her to be there
to fix the old folks something to eat.

She told me just today
that all were treating her well,
I said "By God, they had better,
or they can all just go to hell."

She said, "I know you'd come if I called you
and get here while the dew was still on the grass,
and if they didn't treat me good,
You'd come up here and kick their ass.

You got that right my darling
and they'd all soon learn and see,
that when your messing with Libby
"By God! You are messing with me."

She might look a little weary
maybe a little dark around her eyes,
But inside there lives an angel
all else is just disguise.

ERNEST L. ANDERSON
11/22/03

Mother's Love

Today I walked near my Mother's grave
and looked where she now slept,
I pulled the weeds from around her stone
as my eyes now softly wept.

Just then, as I knelt beside her
with my knee there in the sand,
I had the strangest feeling
that I really felt her hand.

"My son, don't you know I'm with you"?
I thought I heard her say,
"And don't you know that I will love you,
until your dying day?"

"All may leave and forsake you
but, my son, I never will.
I am still right there with you
though I rest with your Dad and Bill."

"You will see me when the violet blooms,
the one you gave to me.
And each morning's sunrise
will bring you memories of me."

"So dry your eyes now, my son
so that you may see and know,
That I am right beside you
when from this place you go."

I slowly turned and walked away
Happy that I could see,
For today I saw my Mother
and she went home with me.

ERNEST L. ANDERSON
11/03/03

Count the Cost

When evening shadows fall
Sandman's bag is filled with sand,
He prepares for his night's duty
to sprinkle it throughout the land.

There is nothing left to do
all the day's words have been said,
I prepare now for slumber
as the pillow receives my head.

Following the Sandman's visit
I count the many sheep,
I contemplate the day
before I go to sleep.

Has my full day been fruitful
or a waste of precious time?
Have my many words been harsh
or were they pleasant and kind?

Did I say only the words
that really needed to be heard?
Did I count the cost
of each and every word?

If the answer were a letter
I hope it would not be mailed,
For when I consider my words
I know that I have failed.

My eyes are now heavy
and feel they want to weep,
Once I have forgiven me
I enter dreamland and find sleep.

ERNEST L. ANDERSON
10/26/03

Do the Things We Should

If we would do the things we should, could we then refrain from those things that we would, should we, could we? I should, and If I could, I would. I find that the thing I would is the thing I should not, yet is the thing I would, if I could. I would not, if I could not, because I should not. Therefore I will not, not because I can not, but because I would not, because I should not. Now, I am glad we got that straight

ERNEST L. ANDERSON
9/20/03

Prisoner of Love

A futile effort will you find
when your release is on your mind,
The freedom sought cannot be found
though no chains around you are bound,
Imprisoned as a hand is to a glove
When you are the prisoner of Love.

ERNEST L. ANDERSON
9/20/03

In Honor of Martha Stuart Oden

If I only had a rocket
or could ride on a shooting star,
I would fly right up to heaven
so I could be there where you are.

We didn't have time enough to dance
or stroll under a moonlit sky,
But while you were here on earth
it was you who had my eye.

I thought of you today
and a tear came to my eye,
It was when I saw a rose petal fall
but a man isn't supposed to cry.

Today I broke the rules
and the floor received my tears,
I would have given anything
to have had you a few more years.

I'll find you there in heaven
you'll be easy for me to see,
I'll just look for the most beautiful angel
that there could ever be.

I didn't tell you that I loved you
we didn't have the time somehow,
But I believe you always knew
that I loved you then and now.

ERNEST L. ANDERSON
9/19/03

Do I Want to Fly?

Do I really want to fly
or only flap my wings?
Do I really want the things
that only flight would bring?

I sit here on the branch
holding on with all my might,
I exercise my wings
as I dream of my first flight.

The sound of the wind excites me
as it whistles through my hair,
the thermals above invite me
to fly up there and share.

I am flapping my wings much harder
but I cannot release my grip,
This will be another night
in which there is no trip.

I'll stay right here and practice
until my wings are strong,
I'll search to find the courage
I hope it won't take long.

Who knows what I'll find
when with eagles I soar above,
It might be just a friend
But then again, it might be love.

ERNEST L. ANDERSON
9/18/03

"Deep Water"

Darling, I'm in deep water
I'm in way over my head,
Please come and throw me a life line
and forgive all the things I said.

I didn't know I had drifted
so far from the shore and your love,
I wait now alone for your answer
with hope as my eyes turn above.

Come quick and throw me a life line
pull me back into your arms,
Let me once more hold and love you
and know the joy of your charms.

I'm sinking fast in deep water
I can see the surface above,
With the cold water all around me
I remember the warmth of your love.

ERNEST L. ANDERSON
9/14/03

Hope Realized

Am I not there?
When in my mind I leave this place
and stroll with you on golden sand,
Where I chance a look at your sweet face,
feel the softness as I grip your hand.

Are you a thief?
When you have stolen my heart
Your only weapon a pouting glance?
Wherein this love received its start
to answer the call of another chance.

What if I go?
When waiting would be as bitter rind
that filled your plate which you must eat.
Where in your mind would solace find
the strength to fight and loneliness defeat?

Should I return?
When you stood with hope waiting for me
If I came back with all my charms,
Where in the distance my coming you see
I would know my hope when you filled my arms.

ERNEST L. ANDERSON
8/23/03

Play the Hand You Were Dealt

I didn't write the book
I just turn the page,
I'm sure it is the same
At this or any age.

I didn't shuffle the cards
and neither did I deal,
I didn't see the deck
when they broke the seal.

I didn't stack the chips
on the table covered with felt,
I just do my best
and play the hand I was dealt.

With a better hand
I could have done more,
We have all heard that excuse
many times before.

I'll just do my best
until my body is old,
I'll play the hand that I was dealt
until I have to fold.

ERNEST L. ANDERSON
8/03/03

If I Were an Octopus

I never thought an octopus
is what I'd like to be,
Until the day I looked at you
and you looked back at me.

And how was I to know
that in that moment then,
You would light the fire of love
which now burns bright within.

So now the flame burns brighter
with the passing of each day,
Funny how one of words
can find little more to say.

Think I'll go to the ocean
and there I'll jump right in,
Try to cool this burning fire
and find an octopus friend.

Maybe he will show me
how I can win your charms,
If I were only an octopus
I could hug you with eight arms.

ERNEST L. ANDERSON
7/30/03

The Want of Wings

Oh for the want of wings
that I might wrap you with my arms,
And thus relieve myself of this hug
you have fully earned with your charms.

To say that it's ok
To hold those memories of the past,
That it took a lifetime for you to make
and throughout the rest of your life will last.

Remember the good times that you had
and be glad that they could last,
Being thankful for that special someone
who was there to share your past.

Look with confidence to the future
as you remember yesterday,
Good things always come to dreamers
who place themselves in dreams way.

Don't be surprised that one day
as you look at the sky above,
You see me flying with my wings
to share with you a hug.

ERNEST L. ANDERSON
7/28/03

Who Are You?

You are the warmth of the sun as it rises over the oceans horizon.
You are the summer shower that takes the heat away.
You are the coolness my hot feet feel when I walk in the surf.
You are the relief after a long run.
You are the cool summer breeze along the shore where I walk.
You are the brilliance in the sunset that I saw tonight.
You are the brightest star in the sky.
You are the comfort for my head as I lie down.
You are the dream that I will dream tonight.

ERNEST L. ANDERSON
7/26/03

Sailors We Are

Ahoy there ye sailor
make fast the ship and sail,
Batten down the hatchs
Prepare for the eastern gale

The wind she is a blowing
A mighty wind is she,
I think I'll have a little nip
and here is one for thee.

The sea spray she is salty
splashing in my face,
If we make it to the shore
It'll be only by his grace.

The storm beat hard our little ship
and freely tossed us about,
Then we broke into the clear
and heard a triumphant shout.

For sailors we are and sailors we'll be
and a hearty lot are we,
I'll soon be there in the pub
have an ale or two with thee.

ERNEST L. ANDERSON
7/12/03

Timeless Beauty

Wherein I was much as you are
with youthful skin and face so fair,
Beautiful in that day without a care,
As for hearts, I broke my share.

Now with years flown swiftly past
Times wrinkles have found their space,
No longer do I give beauty a place,
With the marks of years I can't erase.

Time is relative oh little one
Fret not about your face or skin,
To wear the wrinkles is no sin,
They are where the smiles have been.

When all is said and done
Outward beauty endures but for a while,
Then takes flight as if out of style,
No longer present is the face of a child.

Smile and be glad when you are as I
Remember the places you have been,
Think of the life and the love there has been,
And know that all beauty comes from within.

ERNEST L. ANDERSON
7/12/03

Away with me to Scotland

Away with me to Scotland
the land where I am from,
It was in my dreams I heard her
when my Lassie bid me come.

Out of my way, I have no time
I must sail to her today,
I will pick for her some flowers
that I find along the way.

I cannot wait to get there
and to see my lady fair,
Perhaps I'll even chance a kiss
If I'm feeling brave and dare.

Away with me to Scotland
My true love waits for me,
My arms can't wait to hold her
My eyes can't wait to see.

When I am there I'll ask her
If she will marry me,
And we'll live there forever
in our cottage by the sea.

ERNEST L. ANDERSON
7/12/03

Ultimate Love

Off into the world now I must go
Armed with determination my face aglow
With youthful pride intact I might not fall
As I board the might ship I hear my country's call.
I won't be home for breakfast; don't wait for me.

We sailed from the harbor toward the setting sun
I thought of recent days and smiled at all our fun
Oh, how we loved under blue skies up above
The ring now on your finger will declare our love.
I won't be home for lunch; don't wait for me.

We sailed the mighty sea now in the dark of night
Suddenly a squall appeared no let up was insight
The seas were very high as we were tossed about
The ship was going down of that I had no doubt.
I won't be home for dinner; don't wait for me.

Almost under now as my last breath draws near
I chose your name to be the last word I will ever hear
Weep not for me as I approach heavens towers
Pity those who lived longer and never knew a love like ours.
I won't be home at all; In your heart is where I'll be.

ERNEST L. ANDERSON
6/29/03

What am I?

The veil quickly fell around us and we were plunged into darkness as the glimmer of light faded in the distance behind us until it would be extinguished completely. The fireflies sped by above and on each side of us, as if they were urgently racing in competition to gain the prize of the fading glimmer of light before it was swallowed by the darkness.

As they sped swiftly by, the webbed homes of the permanent inhabitants were visible as they provided a transparent coating which served to subdue the brilliance of the fireflies generated light.

The obnoxious stench of the air was forced into our lungs as we listened to the rumblings beneath us while the white strips blinked continuously at us that were imbedded there.

The undulating, faded scales were seen rapidly proceeded past us overhead and on each side in sync with the fireflies.

In the distance a white beacon could be seen that rapidly increased in size. It made us wonder if the fireflies were not actually running away from the beacon to escape it.

Suddenly we were temporarily blinded as we were catapulted from the darkness and bathed in the surrounding light. We breathed the fresh unforced air once again.

Answer—What you can see and experience when driving through a tunnel.

ERNEST L. ANDERSON
7/02/03

Morning

Awake, Awake
Come feel the morning sun,
Taste the saltiness of the air
a new day has begun.

Walk with me on beaches white
Feel the sand between your toes,
This day our hearts may lead us
to places no one knows.

Where we go matters not
or neither what we do,
as long as you are here with me
and I am there with you.

And now as the horizon
claims the setting sun,
our hearts are joined together
as the two of us become one.

Night shadows now are falling
as we gaze here at the moon,
my heart hears your love calling
another day will be here soon.

ERNEST L. ANDERSON
6/24/03

Who am I?

Who am I
Oh little one?
Can you find me
Under the sun?

I know not time,
I know not speed,
If you follow
I will lead.

I was not born
I was always there,
I can break steel
Cause one to care.

You cannot find me
The lost one is you,
Discover me and see
Beauty in the dew.

I am only pure
When I come from above,
I hope you know me
I am Love, I am Love.

ERNEST L. ANDERSON
6/18/03

Hail to Covington High

Though I left you long ago
there in the Allegheny hills,
Your memory seems to grow sweeter
As I recall the days and thrills.

It was there I found your friendship
in the halls of Cougar land,
Some cheered our team to victory
while some were in the band.

I remember the days at Douthat
the lake's water was very cold,
Where once there lived a mermaid
Or so the story was told.

Though we've gone our separate ways
and are far from the days we knew,
We find our hearts still are bound
as our friendships we renew.

I wonder as I look at your face
If I should just proceed or pass?
Was this someone that I once knew?
Or was it someone from my class?

Though time may dim our memories
even if we lose them in the end,
There is one thing I wish for sure
that you will always be my friend.

Hail to Covington High
and to my friends of long ago,
I hope the love for them within my heart
upon my face will show.

ERNEST L. ANDERSON
6/27/03

Happy Fathers Day to Me

Happy Fathers Day to me
I did all the things I should,
I just couldn't be perfect
Is there anyone who could?

I look to my father in heaven
When perfection is what I wish,
I'm thankful to be his child
When I see his symbol, the fish.

Happy Fathers Day to me
Though you think me all alone,
All of God's Saints are with me
Will be, until I am home.

If only two things I could leave you
It would be two things from above,
Blessings paid by our savior
And the presence of his love.

ERNEST L. ANDERSON
6/15/03

Come Boldly

The road is long with a heavy load
weighted with worldly toil and care,
Too much to carry now all alone
need for solace has come to bare.

It is in your presence that I must go
when all I've done has seemed to fail,
All the roads have met dead ends
bringing my efforts to no avail.

You bid me come and find relief
never again my burdens to meet,
When there with you upon your throne
I leave them all laying at your feet,

With another burden should the need arise
If again I fail I'll do the same,
With head held high I go my way
much lighter now than when I came.

ERNEST L. ANDERSON
6/08/03

The Dawn of Life

The layers of foggy haze rise slowly with beauty and grace having received their existence from the chilly kiss of the morning's dew which blanketed the grass and flowers. Drifting slowly upward, drawn magnetically by the warmth of the days first rays of the sun, the intact blanket accepting the sun's invitation and now separating into segments, giving birth to the figures of steam which swirl and danced individually, ever rising with up lifted arms and swirling into obscurity. It is the dawn of a new day.

Oh Lord, touch those who read these words with your beauty and grace and cover them with your holy spirit as the morning dew blankets the grass and flowers. As they are drawn near to you by the warmth of your love, cause them to separate themselves from the cares of this world and to look to you with opened arms, uplifted in praise and thanksgiving, propelling them into obscurity, and as they decrease, you might increase and the light of the sun may shine through them and be seen by others.

May today be the beginning of a new life.

ERNEST L. ANDERSON
6/07/03

New Life

Oh Lord, touch me with your beauty and grace and cover me with your holy spirit as the morning dew blankets the grass and flowers. As I am drawn near to you by the warmth of your love, cause me to separate myself from the cares of this world and to look to you with opened arms, uplifted in praise and thanksgiving, propelling me into obsurity, and as I decrease, you might increase and the light of the sun may shine through me and be seen by others. It is the beginning of a new life.

ERNEST L. ANDERSON
6/07/03

Dawn

The layers of foggy haze rose slowly with beauty and grace having received their existance from the chilly kiss of the morning's dew which blanketed the grass and flowers. Drifting slowly upward, drawn magnetically by the warmth of the days first rays of the sun, the intact blanket accepted the sun's invitation and now separated into segments, giving birth to the figures of steam which swirled and danced individually, ever rising with up lifted arms and swirling into obscurity. It was the dawn of a new day.

ERNEST L. ANDERSON
6/07/03

Kindred Slave

Ah, for the love of words they gave
I find myself a kindred slave,
To say those things and say them well
Does cause my heart to beat and swell.

To hear Elizabeth's words of love
She shared with Robert from above,
With pen in hand I wish to show
The beauty of the words of Poe.

Yet in my quest how hard I try
Crumpled paper speaks of my sigh,
An empty page will give no light
I hide myself from their sight.

But strive I will until I find
A word or phrase of another kind,
I'll persist with words both strong and bold
Until I am there in their fold.

ERNEST L. ANDERSON
5/05/03

Until

Until the stars fall from the skies
and the mountains are as the plains,
Until the young girls cease their sighs
and the storm clouds bring no rain.

Until the white clouds are no more
and have left the sky of blue,
Until the tide can't kiss the shore
I'll still be loving you.

Until the snow has lost its white
and a circle is no longer round,
Until the birds no more have flight
and lost wings cannot be found.

Until the sun shines in the night
and morning brings no dew,
Until all wrong things are made right
I'll still be loving you.

ERNEST L. ANDERSON
5/10/03

Loving You

Until the stars fall from the skies
and the mountains are as the plains,
Til the young girls cease their sighs
and the storm clouds bring no rain.

Until the white clouds are no more
and have left the sky of blue,
Til the tide won't kiss the shore
I'll still be loving you.

Until the snow has lost its white
and a circle is no longer round,
Til the birds no more have flight
and there is no more sound.

Until the sun shines in the night
and morning brings no dew,
With all these things in sight
I'll still be loving you.

ERNEST L. ANDERSON
5/10/03

The Beacon of your Love

You've taken all my sunshine
leaving the overcast sky,
I won't stand around and whine
or ask the reason why.

I only know its dark now
where the light had just been,
I won't ask why or how
in the message that I send.

I don't need to know the reason
that the day has turned to night,
It could be just the season
to make the wrong turn from right.

As I travel thru the dark now
down the path I cannot see,
I'll get back to you somehow
with your love a beacon for me.

ERNEST L. ANDERSON
5/09/03

The Window of Your Soul

No words are needed
in the closeness of this moment,
As your eyes reveal to mine
this love that heaven sent.

A heartbeat away
from your joyous sighs,
As I peer into your soul
through the window of your eyes.

What others have only dreamed
I find I now possess,
Nothing more is needed
Nothing more or less.

Paradise was tasted
from the very first glance,
Surely preordained
and not by chance.

Silence is golden indeed
words useless I find,
My soul hears your heart
and your soul hears mine.

ERNEST L. ANDERSON
5/03/03

True Love

True love was elusive
Until the day that I found you,
But now our hearts are as close
As the roses kiss, by the morning dew.

It seems I never could find
the one my empty heart sought,
Now it cannot contain
the joy your love has brought.

The treasure of your love
has brought the joy I now embrace,
No more to search for rainbows end
My eye tasted the beauty of your face.

I found in my heart that day
a place where you can reside,
A place apart from the whole world
where we alone can hide.

Then I'll have you with me
every moment of the day,
My treasure in safekeeping
we can be on our way.

ERNEST L. ANDERSON
5/03/03

The Garden

This moment in time in the garden
in the midst of the azaleas there,
The sweet scent of their perfume
wafting gently through the air.

Since spring has finally come
with the flowers now in full bloom,
It causes me to search my memory
and for this garden to make room.

As my eye drinks in the beauty
of the flowers in their various hues,
The azaleas hold on tightly
to the blooms they soon must lose.

Later on this winter
when the snow is on the ground,
I'll return there to my memory
and see the beautiful garden I found.

ERNEST L. ANDERSON
4/30/03

My Prayer

I know that you are hurting now
as your friend I feel your pain,
I can't feel it just like you do
but I feel it, just the same.

I wish that I could do something
just to let you know I care,
Know that I am thinking of you
and in that way, I am there.

As you go through this time of sorrow
and your numbness turns to grief,
I pray the comforter will be with you
and give you his relief.

Lean now on God's shoulder
and in his love abide,
For you will see your loved one
when you too, reach the other side.

ERNEST L. ANDERSON
3/1103

Nothing Left to Lose or Gain

Now there is nothing to lose
and nothing to gain,
Looks like everything
will just remain the same.

Since you said goodbye
leaving only this pain,
Turning all of our sunshine
Into the falling rain

I held you so tight
when our love was brand new,
Now all that has changed
and I'm feeling so blue.

What went so wrong
that we couldn't repair?
I guess it all means
That you just didn't care.

So I go on my way
and deal with this pain
With nothing left to lose
and nothing to gain.

ERNEST L. ANDERSON
3/09/03

The Horrors of War

The horrors of war
are before our eyes,
Amid the pain and sorrow
and desperate sighs.

Our hearts fill with pride
as our warriors do their best,
We hurt as a mother grieves
when she lays her son to rest.

The horrors of war
continue through out the night,
For a cause that is just
to remove despair and put hope in their sight.

Many lived their entire life
under the oppressive fear,
Their hearts now fill with joy
as the day of freedom draws near.

Not that we really knew them
as our relative or friend,
But because of our love for freedom
Our soldiers we send.

When we see their little children
and look into their eyes,
Our hearts fill with compassion
and we're touched, as the little one cries.

Who can oppose the war
and without feeling turn their back?
In the face of an oppressed people
Who have known nothing but lack.

It is for them that I have pity
and pray to God above,
That he will take their ignorance
and replace it with his love.

ERNEST L. ANDERSON
4/11/03

The Effect of Music

And as he sat there listening to the music, it seemed to encompass the entire area and all that were within its range of sound. Entering thru the ears and taking captive his very soul as the sounds resonated throughout his being. The uplifted feeling of the adrenalin rush which it caused to energize him released his spirit to soar as if on wings of eagles. Arriving there in what seemed to be another dimension and time he sat totally enthralled as he absorbed the energizing forces projected from the music. Nothing was impossible at that time, at those heights, when the creativity flowed within him as the enveloping music merged his spirit with the ebb and flow of the music.

ERNEST L. ANDERSON
1/31/04

Searching Eye

To take your presence from my eye
Would surely start my heart to sigh,
Being startled so it would begin to leap
My searching eye would find no sleep.

In days before when we were there
I'd run my fingers thru your hair,
And whisper softly in your ear
All the things you loved to hear.

Now that is gone and in the past
It was a dream that could not last,
Leaving my heart now in history
Found in its place, this mystery.

I play the hand which I was dealt
And move beyond the things I felt,
Give no thought of the tears I cried
Wait to see you, on the other side.

ERNEST L. ANDERSON
3/03/03

Trade In

I have two sister's that are funny
And let me tell you, they make money,
Sometimes I email them until I am dizzy
Which brings up my other sister, Issie.

They all it seems are real busy
To catch them is sometimes a chore,
But I found a way out of this tizzy
When I went to the used sister's store.

I have three busy sister's here for a trade
Do you think we can make a deal?
I have two over there in the shade
And as to their unbusiness, I'll place my seal.

The plan was laid and the deal was made
So I gave the three for the two,
I'll always regret the price I paid
And now I'm wondering just what I should do.

Now I have found Lakeysha and Carmeletta
But I was thinking that I might have done betta,
When I opened the living room door
And in came 10 kids tracking mud on the floor.

Now these kids are driving me crazy
And Lakeysha and Carmeletta are lazy,
They have eaten until my cubboard is bare
Before I could even fill out this form for welfare.

I know what I'll do come Monday
If I can only survive through this Sunday,
Theres one thing I'll do for shore
Head back to the used sisters store.

ERNEST L. ANDERSON
3/08/03

Gone and Yet Here

Gone and yet here, I know not why you left me
I only know that you are gone
And now this burden is heavy I see
to carry on my back, hither and yawn.

Was the grass across the fence that green?
Or his magnetic pull that strong?
That you could go and leave me clean
Turning what was right into wrong?

I follow you not, for the road is long
My heart turns you loose and sets you free,
Loud and clear, I sing a new song
For another love, is waiting for me.

I wish you well, as you go your way
Not all is lost as we end this affair,
The memories of you with me will stay
Of that I'm sure you are aware.

ERNEST L. ANDERSON
3/01/03

Whispers from the Hills

The top of the mountain is where I stood
and witnessed the vast array of beauty there,
My mind seemed absent of just the right words
their majestic beauty could possibly share.

Speechless in awe I stood before them
my eyes enthralled by the majestic view,
The only thing that would make it better
would be sharing this enchanted time with you.

How majestic and how grand they are
these hills standing so proudly before me,
Their vibrant beauty so graciously given
the wave of ridges for my eyes to see.

I hear the soft Whispers from the Hills
their silent beauty given to enhance,
Magnetically they draw my eyes to them
Taking possession from the very first glance.

No words will ever be spoken or heard
which will give justice to these joyous thrills,
It must be felt with the heart, when you hear and see
The Whispers from the Hills.

ERNEST L. ANDERSON
2/22/03

Chance or Fate

Just by chance I saw you there
Dancing gracefully on the floor,
In a moments time my life had changed
I'd now have you for evermore.

Or was it fate when in that glance,
your eyes met mine and seem to say,
"I'll love you forever" whether fate or chance
Leave me never no not for a day.

I saw your smile from across the room
your inviting eyes made me so sure,
As I met you there and took your hand
we danced our first of many more.

Our love took root and began to grow
You were surly sent from heavens gate,
As long as you're here it matters not
If it was by chance or if by fate.

ERNEST L. ANDERSON
2/16/03

Memories that Won't Die

I tried to drown all my troubles
in that bottle that I held so tight,
I can see that they all survived
when your memory returned tonight.

I've got lonesome on top of misery
they won't leave me alone tonight,
I tried everything to hide from them
but when I look they're still in sight.

When you left I felt so lonesome
guess I'll always wear this frown,
I think I'll get another bottle
fight the memories that just won't drown.

Yes I've played the fool and lost
this story has been told before,
How the memory of you has hurt me
since the day you walked out the door.

I've got to drown these memories
even if it takes all night,
I must put them all to rest
and get them forever out of my sight.

ERNEST L. ANDERSON
2/08/03

Regret

When he held you in his arms
as you danced there on the floor,
To my mind returned the memory
when my arms were there before.

I returned there in my mind
to the times when we danced till dawn,
Now its another's arms that hold you
you are the prize that he has won.

Why did I ever lose you
How could I have been so blind?
I didn't mean to leave you lonesome
to treat you mean or be unkind.

You were all that I ever wanted
No man could wish for more,
But I knew that I had lost you
The night you slowly closed the door.

Now I sit here all alone
Just my memories and I remain,
and as I try to drown the sorrow
I find I'm the only one to blame.

ERNEST L. ANDERSON
2/08/03

My Trouble

Although you left me for another
and my heart yearns for you still,
I won't share with you my trouble
as you give in to his will.

I won't share with you my trouble
Though it hurts me more each day,
There is no salve or ointment
for the words you failed to say.

I'll just hang onto the memories
which is all you left behind,
I won't share with you my trouble
as you see what you can find.

Just remember when you are lonely
and the snow is on the ground,
I didn't share with you my trouble
and now I'm not around.

I won't share with you my trouble
and only one thing more I'd say,
Don't come crying on my shoulder
when your friend has gone his way.

ERNEST L. ANDERSON
2/08/03

I'll Love you in Any Season

If winter is now upon us
Can spring be far behind?
Now we seek heat from the stove
Then the suns warmth we'll find.

The creator knows best
of his scheme in all things,
We only guess what he knows
and what spring will finally bring.

When the snow has all melted
and the cold is no more,
There is really only one thing
that I can say for sure.

Though the season has changed
from the cold winter to spring,
My love for you is the same
No matter what spring will bring.

I'll love you in any season
no matter if its cold or hot,
Thru the snow storm or the rainfall
I'll love you, no matter what.

ERNEST L. ANDERSON
1/28/03

Resurrected Slave

Did I not suffer enough
when I suffered way back then?
Your attempt to resurrect me
will meet a futile end.

It was I who was the slave
took the stripes upon my back,
You know not of what you speak
for you there is no lack.

You talk of how you suffer
how things just are not right,
How narrow is your vision
when you only see black or white?

My life I lived with courage
my pain was felt without,
But always on the inside
Love reigned for all no doubt.

Make peace with your maker
refine the things you've said,
Live your life here and now
and let us slaves just remain dead.

Just when I got settled
and accepted my place in history,
You come along and dig up my bones
and only add to our misery.

There is peace here where I am
I'd rather be in my grave,
Than be pulled from a history book
to be a resurrected slave.

ERNEST L. ANDERSON
2/01/03

Madonna

He walked with purpose down the often trodden path, claimed as his own in his youth, and somewhat over grown now with the tall grass that gave evidence of its reclamation. His hatless head allowed the summer breeze to tousle his white hair against his leathery face as his blue eyes read the signposts of rocks and trees projecting on the screen of his mind, a picture of the landscape as it was in the days of his youth a half century ago. Arriving at the creek, he focused on the pristine water as it flowed slowly with grace revealing the washed pebbles resting on its bottom. Then to his private bank he strolled just off the creek where he scooped up a double handful of the red clay. Now placing the clay on the big oak stump he dutifully walked to the creek and scooping up a double handful of water, he returned and mixed the water with the clay. He heard the voice of the white flowers of the *Lilium Candidum* as they silently revealed to him what his creation would be. The size of the mud pile increased as he added more water and clay until his eye said enough. The statue began to take shape when on bended knee, as if praying, he knelt before the stump and his gnarled hands molded and shaped the mixture. Methodically and with purpose he followed the blueprint in his mind. He extended the usefulness of a fallen twig by using it as a tool to shape the delicate features of her face. Nearly finished, he returned to the creek, and washed his hands while his eyes never left her. He returned with wet hands and smoothed the creation into being. Satisfied finally with his efforts, he returned to the path and retraced his steps with her cradled gingerly in his arm. Arriving home he placed her on the mantle in the center where the warmth of the fireplace would slowly cure her. He slowly withdrew from her and sat in his chair across the room. There he gazed upon her. He closed his eyes and could see her still. When he opened his eyes, his mind said *yes, she is just as I saw her yesterday from this place.*

ERNEST L. ANDERSON
1/31/03

The Dawn

The last moments of the night struggle to survive, wishing to extend its allotted time, and to continue to hold captive to the darkness, all who are under its veil.

The sun, however, not welcoming the encroachment on its time, slowly and with precision, uses the pointed tip of its knife to pierce the darkness, thus sending the sun's first penetrating rays cascading into the reluctantly yielding blackness of the night. The birth of the morning continues as the pierced area widens and the sunrise begins by announcing her presence with a dazzling display of beauty as she triumphantly claims her time, leaving in her wake, swirling figures of steam created by the dew as it is awakened and rises to escape the warming rays of the sun. The Spring flowers begin to open up, giving the appearance of weeping as the remaining dew drops fall from their petals, while they receive the nourishment the sun provides. The quietness of the dawn provides a peaceful respite, though short in duration, it soon fades into obscurity, as the inhabitants awaken to the new day, destroying the silent serenity with their movements.

ERNEST L. ANDERSON
1/24/04

Help Another Rose to Bloom

When I first saw you I knew my search was over
A search I thought would surly never end,
And Darling now you've left me for another
I pack my bags and let my new search now begin.

Darling please, just spare me all the reasons
No more pain can in my heart have room,
I'll just go and pick up all the pieces
and maybe someday help another rose to bloom.

I know that I will never find another
That I can love the way I loved you true,
And as dark clouds now close in around me
All roads in my memory lead me back to you.

Darling I know that when my search is over
and I can give a new love now a start,
I'll do my best to weed out all the trouble
and help another rose to bloom, in her heart.

ERNEST L. ANDERSON
6/06/03

The Mighty Oak

Tree, tall and strong, there on the hill
Would you now speak, had you the will?
Or repeat your silence as before
And guard your secrets even more?

Much you've heard, standing near that house
Always listening, quiet as a mouse,
Quite a story, you could tell no doubt
Had you a tongue to let it out.

You've seen them all, both young and old
Through all seasons, warm and cold,
You watched Tommy fall from that thick limb
Saw his mother run to comfort him.

You held the chain for the children's swing
Heard small voices of laughter ring,
Gave squirrels and birds space for a home
Training limbs for their young to roam.

There wasn't much that you would miss
Even saw Sally get her first kiss,
Watched when Billy carved her a heart
Heard them vow never to part.

As I look at you now from my window above
I don't know why, but I feel love,
Isn't that what you gave, though you never spoke?
Isn't that why they call you, The Mighty Oak?

ERNEST L. ANDERSON
1/26/04

Unknown Soldier

What place is this that I have found?
A soldier's tomb there on this ground,
He has no name there carved in stone
No friends or relatives to be known.

Some mother's son he was for sure
raised with a love strong and pure,
Whose silent tears now water the earth
as she recalls the day of his birth.

Too young to die, it seemed a waste
No one knows the hell he faced,
He gave his life so we'd be free
An awesome thing for you and me.

His body lies cold now in his grave
Has taken his place among the brave,
I thought as I gazed, what can I do
to repay this soldier what he is due?

I can respect our flag, when to it, I am near
I can thank our soldiers for facing our fear,
I can love my country, for which he stood
I can do good for another, just as he would.

I can pray for peace, and our soldiers' return
to a hero's welcome, which they all have earned,
I can pray that the enemy might see the light
and learn to love instead of fight.

ERNEST L. ANDERSON
1/24/04

I Just Came to Dance

Don't dance with me when you're thinking of him
I'd rather not dance if he's there on your mind,
Just once try to forget and give my love a chance
May I have just one dance and true love you will find.

I just came here to dance I didn't know I'd fall in love
I saw you once before as he held you oh so tight;
Then I made a mistake when I looked into your eyes
And when I left lonesome went with me that night.

I've dreamed of this dance so many lonely nights
Tonight was my chance as I found you by the door,
Don't think of him as it's my arms you now fill
Just hold on tight as I twirl you on the floor.

Now I've danced my way there in your heart
Your smile just told me what your heart had said,
When I leave tonight you'll be right there by my side
leaving my footprints and lonesome I have shed.

ERNEST L. ANDERSON
6/06/03

Footprints

May the footprints that I leave
from strife and sorry lead,
And to the comfort of another
reaping the harvest of bad seed.

Through my eyes may he see forward
when the future through his looks grim,
May he see the light of hope ahead
though it be small and dim.

May I help to remove his burden
that he carries upon his back,
May I fill the empty basket
and give where there is lack.

When his day of struggle is over
and he lies down in his bed,
May the words I've said bring comfort
and be the pillow for his head.

May I feel the pain of others
who are brave and do not cry,
And remember that where they are
but for His grace am I.

ERNEST L. ANDERSON
8/02/03

Grandmother's Timeless Beauty

Wherein I was much as you are
With youthful skin and face so fair,
Beautiful in that day without a care,
As for hearts, I broke my share.

Now with years flown swiftly past
Times wrinkles have found their space,
No longer do I give beauty a place,
With the marks of years I can't erase.

Time is relative oh little one
Fret not about your face or skin,
To wear the wrinkles is no sin,
They are where the smiles have been.

When all is said and done
Outward beauty endures but for a while,
Then takes flight as if out of style,
No longer present is the face of a child.

Smile and be glad when you are as I
Remember the places you have been,
Think of the life and the love there has been,
And know that all beauty comes from within.

ERNEST L. ANDERSON
7/12/03

Music

You fill my heart with Joy
causing it to overflow,
You are there to raise my head
when I am feeling low.

You are right there with me
in the cold and lonely night,
An ever present comfort
when all is not right.

You give my heart its wings
and let me with eagles soar,
You will always come through
when I need that something more.

With all things that you are
your melody fills each day,
You are the music in my life
forever there to stay.

ERNEST L. ANDERSON
9/09/03

Live Above It

Though my heart is ever breaking
and the pain I would not share,
I choose to be one of love
and help other's burdens bare.

This rule of life I give you
that all who live must learn,
It is only when we give
that we can receive then in return.

Though others wish to hurt you
and pile burdens on your back,
Give to them your blessing
and never will you lack.

Just always live above it
when the storm clouds form above,
Nothing can defeat you
When your heart is filled with love.

ERNEST L. ANDERSON
8/02/03

If you try to hide, I will find you

I will see you in the rose
that I just picked today,
You are there
I hear the words that you would say.

You are the freshness
just after the rain,
You are there
as I walk down memory lane.

You are the brightest star
in the star filled sky,
You are there
shining to please my eye.

You are the melody
that the orchestra plays,
You are there
bringing inspiration that stays.

I will find you
even in the dark of night,
You are there
as a distant beacon's light.

I will find you
below or above,
Nothing can separate me
from your love.

ERNEST L. ANDERSON
7/22/03

Hope Realized

Am I not there?
When in my mind I leave this place
and stroll with you on golden sand,
Where I chance a look at your sweet face

feel the softness as I grip your hand.
Are you a thief?
When you have stolen my heart
Your only weapon a pouting glance?

Wherein this love received its start
to answer the call of another chance.
What if I go?
When waiting would be as bitter rind

that filled your plate which you must eat,
Where in your mind would solace find
the strength to fight and loneliness defeat?
Should I return?

When you stood with hope waiting for me
If I came back with all my charms,
Where in the distance my coming you see
I would know my hope when you filled my arms.

ERNEST L. ANDERSON
8/23/03

Hailey's Comet

The streak in the nighttime sky
had my attention, once it caught my eye
It was Haley's Comet that had sped past
Leaving a white tail that would not last

It blew a kiss toward earth as it went by
bounced off the Rockies, leaving them to sigh
The kiss traveled on as it began to rain
Into the heartland through amber waves of grain

Soon it was past there and headed east
Wheat fields lay bowed, as the wind had not ceased, It caused a big breeze on the shore as it swiftly flew by Blew over the sand dunes and created waves eight feet high.

On out to shore and across the sea
Come morning, The British Isles is where that kiss will be,
The breeze from it blowing my wee bonnie's brown hair
As it waves to Ole Scotland, then proceeds with flair.

It made it to London, and through the fog
Then took its last breath and lay by the bog,
Its pucker power gone, they would remember that day
When Haley blew a kiss, then flew on its way.

ERNEST L. ANDERSON
8/27/03

I Can Hear Your Love Calling

With every drop of rain that falls
Every song the Robin sings,
I can hear your love calling
and feel the joy it brings.

I can hear your love calling
in the midst of the noisy crowd,
Nothing drowns out the voice I hear
the one that's made me proud.

With every wave that tumbles in
then rests there on the shore,
I watch and wish for a bigger heart
so I could love you more.

I can hear your love calling
Its sweet music fills my ears,
Soon my arms will hold you
while I love away the tears.

ERNEST L. ANDERSON
8/31/03

The Window of Your Soul

No words are needed
in the closeness of this moment,
As your eyes reveal to mine
this love that heaven sent.

A heartbeat away
from your joyous sighs,
As I peer into your soul
through the window of your eyes.

What others have only dreamed
I find I now possess,
Nothing more is needed
Nothing more or less.

Paradise was tasted
from the very first glance,
Surely preordained
and not by chance.

Silence is golden indeed
words useless I find,
My soul hears your heart
and your soul hears mine.

ERNEST L. ANDERSON
5/03/03

The Passion of the Poet

The passion of the poet a consuming fire
will forever burn when once its lit,
Burning within every waking hour
Arranging words until they fit.

Creating with words a story to tell
Pathos of yearnings to tell it well,
Bearing his soul giving his gift
With hope when read will bring a lift.

To draw one up reveals his ploy
As if by a magnet where there is joy,
To enter there the soft pure light
Earthly burdens far from sight.

To leave one better than they were found
By using his tools paper and pen,
The music of his soul the only sound
A choir of angels ushers in.

Held captive by words he continues to write
Often all day until late at night,
To bring to you the fruit of his hands
With hope your vision and life expands.

ERNEST L. ANDERSON
1/31/04

Love Enough for Tomorrow

Do you love me enough for tomorrow?
I know how you feel today,
Could you deal with the pain and sorrow?
If we each went our own way?

Forever still means a lifetime
There can be no other way,
If you can't love me more than sometime
There is nothing left to say.

Why can't you love me always?
The way that I'll always love you?
Why is it just another phase
Like the others that you've been through?

If you can't love me enough for tomorrow
After all that we've been through,
Though my heart is filled with sorrow
I must say goodbye to you.

Darling, please think it over
Tonight when you're all alone,
If you find enough love for tomorrow
I'll be here to welcome you home.

ERNEST L. ANDERSON
2/01/04

The Birth

How could it be that before us we see
this virgin lying here so pale?
How could it be that she could conceive
and is now here in travail?

They tried and failed, the wise men knew not
the meaning of the ongoing events,
The Ladies just smiled at the looks they got
but gave no clues or hints.

"Could it be a miracle or maybe a hex
that has brought this occurrence about?"
"A miracle Yes, they said, but surely no hex"
as they swelled from withholding their shout.

Just then came a groan as he became known
they watched with nothing to say,
They soon had wrapped the little boy
and in his mothers arm's he lay.

The birth of The King, the miracle did bring
an event which would never repeat,
"Our Savior has come" they began to sing
as he lay there at their feet.

ERNEST L. ANDERSON
7/25/03

The Power of a Smile

The power of a smile is a curious thing
Considering the contagious joy it can bring,
It can also cause one to scratch his head
When trying to decipher what a smile has said.

Often not easy to know what was meant
Or understand with certainty the sender's intent,
Sometimes fleeting framed in a quick glance
Some so subtle they are caught only by chance.

Often they are given with nothing in mind
Just offered freely to be considerate and kind,
Sometimes useful with a word of good cheer
To help a small child chase away a tear.

I hope that your life, in the midst of the wiles
Will be happy and fruitful abundant with smiles,
Don't keep your smiles just consider them lent
Return them all to from where they were sent.

ERNEST L. ANDERSON
2/14/04

Completed Book

Staring at a blank page before him, the withdrawal now moves in, as if it was a dark cloud, filled with rain, which has now come to destroy the serenity and peace of the cloudless blue sky. So the book is now completed, and he waits for its return from the editor.

Writing is as oxygen to him that he must breathe in order to live.

Now, with the book completed, pathos of sorrow replace those loved ones whom he has nurtured and fed, as they are wrenched from his heart, and now go to serve others, leaving in their wake, severed ties and broken bonds to fill the wasteland which once was his heart.

Realizing that every book with a beginning must have an ending seems little consolation or comfort, at this time of separation, when those created, are separated from their creator, never to meet again those who were created, and yet took on such reality that they lived and breathed the same air as the one who created them. Unaware and unconcerned of the plight of their creator, they move swiftly to fulfill the destiny for which they were created.

Yearnings for those now gone, to return and fill his lungs with oxygen, go unfulfilled, as the dark clouds now invite all of their relatives to join in covering any remaining ray of sunshine, and thus, leave him in total darkness.

Struggling in the darkness for his pen, he hurriedly begins to write and to give a new book its beginning pages. Oxygen begins to fill his lungs once more, as the storm clouds overhead are dissipated by the sun, as it streams thru the clouds, accompanied by the refreshing breeze which blows them away.

New characters are created and begin to breathe, taking on personalities and providing fellowship and love for their creator, who having replaced his heavy burden with themselves, he can now breathe deeply and live again.

ERNEST L. ANDERSON
12/09/03

The Ant

What can we say then
when we consider the ant?
Should we expound on the things they can do
or mention the things they can't?

Guides, overseers and rulers
are things that they have not,
Wisdom and devotion to duty
are some things that they have got.

If the sluggard would only watch and learn
that they were not hindered by size,
He could exchange his time in slumber
and walk with those who are wise.

He could soon escape his poverty
and his want would be no more.
If he considered how they worked
to lay up their food in store.

When the winter winds are blowing
and the ants are snug below,
The sluggard must eat the fruit
of the seeds he did not sow.

While they eat the food they gathered
and rest warm upon their bed,
The sluggard is silent above them
Lying stiff, cold and dead.

ERNEST L. ANDERSON
7/30/03

Thoughts of Spring

With the fields now covered with snow's pure white
The barn's icicles reflect the light,
In winter's grip, we are all held tight
Our thoughts soon turn to spring.
The renewing warmth it will bring.

The cold winds blowing cut to the bone
Trudging through snow to feed the roan
His whinny seems to say "Don't leave me alone"
Spring seems a long way off.
Dark clouds now circle aloft.

Into the barn I remove him now
Shielded and warmed from the wind's mighty howl
As much comfort tonight as the stall will allow
Spring flowers return to our mind's sight
Lush meadows fill the roan's dreams tonight.

Now, as the pillow receives my head
I think of the roan resting in his bed
In out of the cold and fully fed
I think of spring now on its way
As the sandman quietly ends the day.

ERNEST L. ANDERSON
2/14/04

The Moon

Oh moon above so full tonight
Freely giving an abundance of light,
Where you are going no one knows
With silence following the path you chose.

How many lovers have spoken to you?
Wanting your secrets opening hearts to you?
If you could speak; what would you say?
Would you speak of love that has come your way?

Remaining there in silence in the sky above
I thought I saw you smile when I spoke of love,
You look so stately in your place there in the sky
Looking down on us with your all knowing eye.

You won't share your secrets nor wisdom will you lend
For silence is your forte on that you will not bend,
I can still enjoy your beauty and count you as my friend
Because I know you've kept my secrets; on that I can depend.

ERNEST L. ANDERSON
2/14/04

Your Love

Of you there is no equal
A precious jewel so rare,
A book without a sequel
None to you could compare.

You are the breeze that fills my sail
The picture of beauty and grace,
The beauty of the rose is pale
When held beside your face.

There is no span or measure
Which can quantify your love,
You are my greatest treasure
Surely descended from above.

To what can you compare?
Nothing earthbound anyone knows,
You're the fairest angel of the fair
Whose love just grows and grows.

Your love is like a river
Where the peaceful waters flow,
Cupid's arrows fill my quiver
As I aim my trusty bow.

ERNEST L. ANDERSON
2/22/04

Ernest Anderson

www.ingramcontent.com/pod-product-compliance
Lightning Source LLC
Chambersburg PA
CBHW022012120526
44592CB00034B/792